Creating Rain

Published in the United States of America by Cherry Lake Publishing
Ann Arbor, Michigan
www.cherrylakepublishing.com

Reading Adviser: Marla Conn MS, Ed., Literacy specialist, Read-Ability, Inc.
Book Design: Jennifer Wahi
Illustrator: Jeff Bane

Library of Congress Cataloging-in-Publication Data

Names: Rowe, Brooke, author.
Title: Creating rain / Brooke Rowe.
Description: Ann Arbor : Cherry Lake Publishing, [2016] | Series: My science
  fun | Audience: K to grade 3.
Identifiers: LCCN 2015049394| ISBN 9781634710275 (hardcover) | ISBN
  9781634712255 (pbk.) | ISBN 9781634711265 (pdf) | ISBN 9781634713245
  (ebook)
Subjects: LCSH: Condensation--Juvenile literature. | Precipitation
  (Meteorology)--Juvenile literature. | Science--Study and teaching
  (Elementary)--Juvenile literature.
Classification: LCC QC924.7 .R69 2016 | DDC 551.57/4--dc23
LC record available at http://lccn.loc.gov/2015049394

Printed in the United States of America
Corporate Graphics Inc.

About the illustrator: Jeff Bane and his two business partners own a studio along the American River in Folsom, California, home of the 1849 Gold Rush. When Jeff's not sketching or illustrating for clients, he's either swimming or kayaking in the river to relax.

table of contents

Asking Questions 4

Science Fun 10

Glossary & Index 24

Science Notes

Creating Rain explores the water cycle. In this experiment, wet soil is sealed in a bag and left in the sunlight. Over time, the natural processes of evaporation, condensation, and precipitation are observed.

Do you like rainy days?
It's fun to play in the rain.
You can jump in puddles.
You can make a big splash.

Rainy days are fun. But do you ever wonder where rain comes from? Or where it goes?

What if we made a model of rain? Do you think it would help us understand?

Let's find out!

- ½ cup of dirt

- Ziplock sandwich bag

- Spray bottle of water

- Tape

- Window

You will need these things

1/2 CUP

Put the dirt in the sandwich bag.

Use the spray bottle to moisten the dirt.

Zip up the sandwich bag.

Tape the bag to a window. Make sure the window gets plenty of sun.

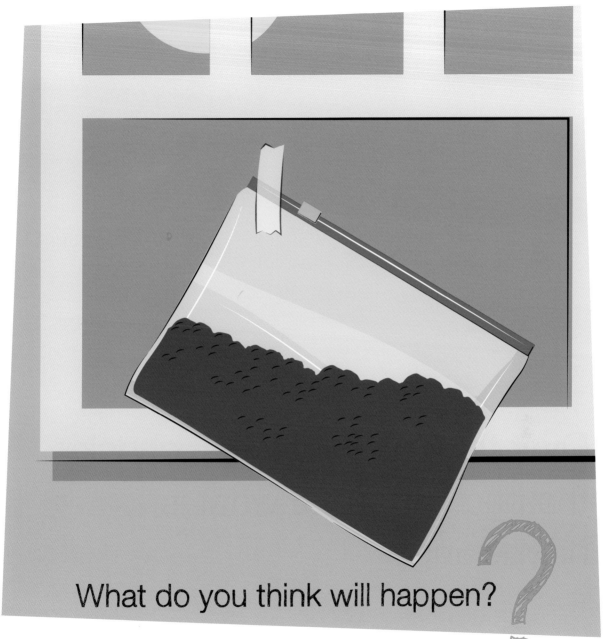

What do you think will happen?

Over the next few days, check the bag. **Observe** what is happening.

What do you see?

The water leaves the dirt.
It becomes **droplets**.
The droplets fall on the dirt.

Why do you think this is?

Continue to watch the bag. **Compare** what happens on sunny and cloudy days.

Good job. You're done!
Science is fun!

What new questions do you have?

glossary

compare (kum-PAIR) to see what is alike or different about two or more things

droplets (DRAHP-lets) very small drops of liquid

observe (uhb-ZURV) to watch something carefully

index

dirt, 12–13, 18
droplets, 18

rain, 4–6
    making, 10–20

sandwich bags,
    12–13, 14–15
spray bottle, 12
sun, 14, 20

supplies, 10–11

water, 18